FIRST
ANIMAL
PICTURE ATLAS

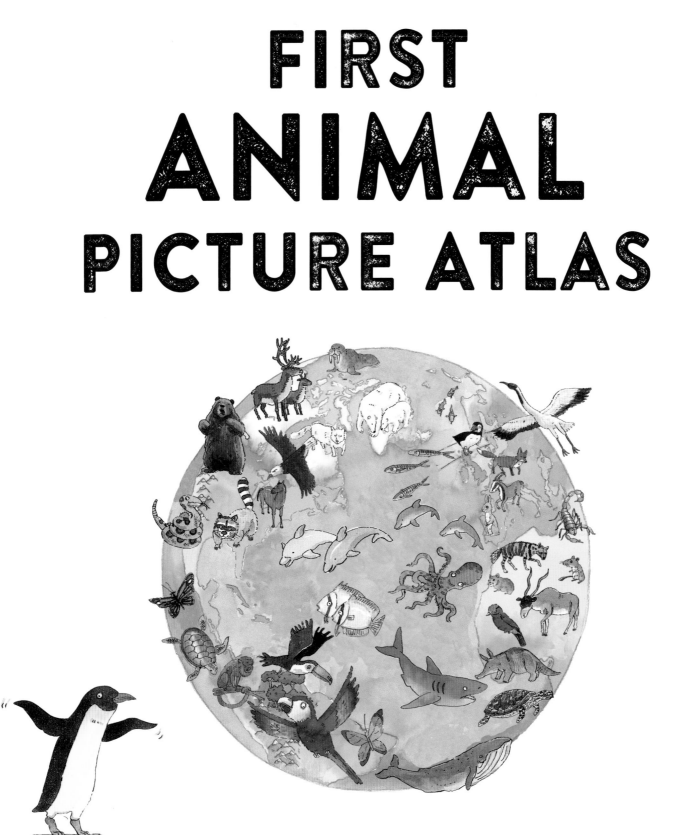

Written by Deborah Chancellor

Illustrated by Anthony Lewis

KINGFISHER
LONDON & NEW YORK

KINGFISHER
LONDON & NEW YORK

Copyright © Macmillan Publishers International Ltd 2006, 2019
This edition published in 2019 by Kingfisher
120 Broadway, New York, NY 10271
Kingfisher is an imprint of Macmillan Children's Books, London
All rights reserved.

Distributed in the U.S. and Canada by Macmillan,
120 Broadway, New York, NY 10271

Library of Congress Cataloging-in-Publication data

Chancellor, Deborah.
The kingfisher first animal picture atlas/Deborah Chancellor.—1st ed.
p. cm.
Includes index.
1. Animals—Pictorial works—Juvenile literature. 2. Habitat
(Ecology)—Pictorial works—Juvenile literature. 3. Zoogeography—
Pictorial works—Juvenile literature. I. Title.
QL49.C47 2006
590–dc22   2005033207

ISBN: 978-0-7534-7527-0

Illustrations by Antony Lewis
Cover Design by Laura Hall

Kingfisher books are available for special promotions and
premiums. For details contact: Special Markets Department,
Macmillan, 120 Broadway, New York, NY 10271

For more information please visit
www.kingfisherbooks.com

Printed in Malaysia
9 8 7 6 5 4 3 2 1
1TR/0919/WKT/UG/128MA

CONTENTS

KEY

country border

state border

disputed border

river

lake

Desert Dry area with sand and rocks

Dry grassland Flat, grassy plains with only a few trees

Temperate grassland Flat, grassy plains with some trees

Forest Areas with many trees

Mountains Tall hills and rugged land

Tundra Flat area close to the Arctic with frozen ground and no trees

Ice and snow Place where ice and snow cover the ground

Seas and oceans Salty water that covers most of Earth

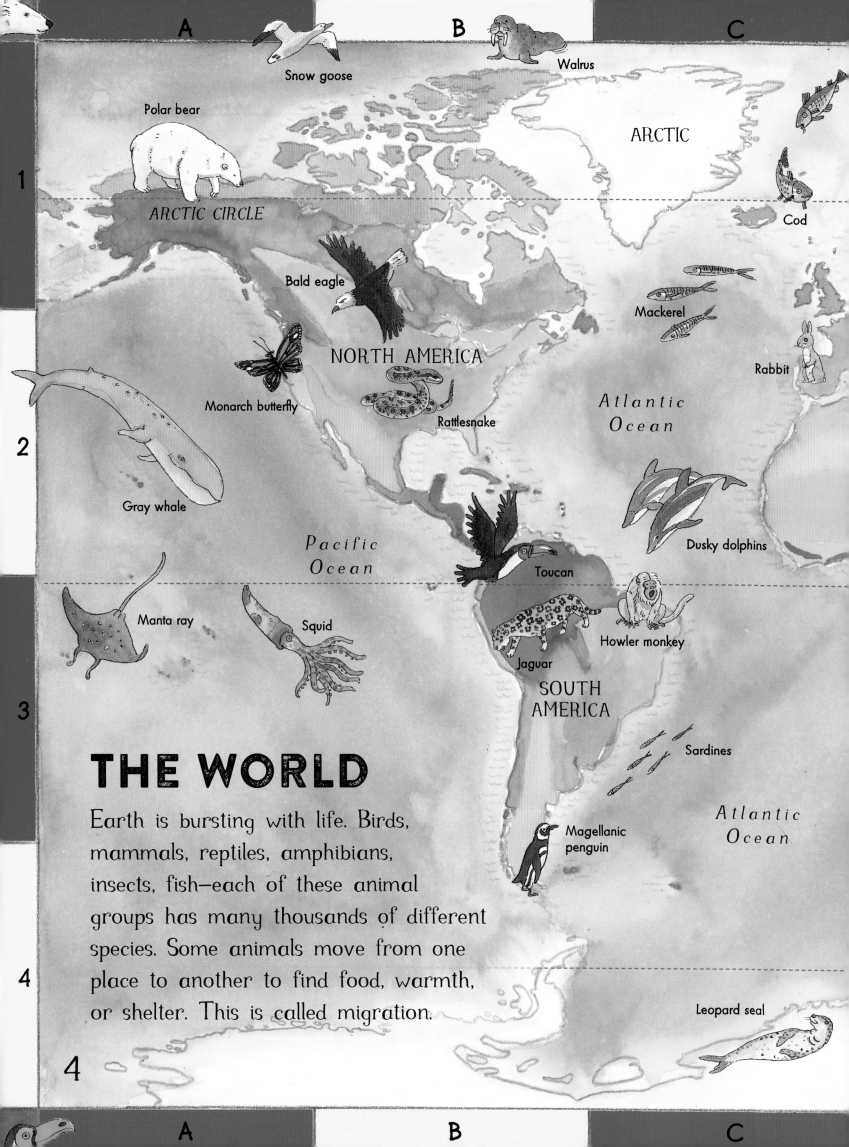

A   B   C

Snow goose

Walrus

Polar bear

ARCTIC

1

ARCTIC CIRCLE

Cod

Bald eagle

Mackerel

Monarch butterfly

NORTH AMERICA

Rabbit

Atlantic Ocean

Rattlesnake

2

Gray whale

Dusky dolphins

Pacific Ocean

Toucan

Manta ray

Squid

Howler monkey

Jaguar

SOUTH AMERICA

3

Sardines

THE WORLD

Earth is bursting with life. Birds, mammals, reptiles, amphibians, insects, fish—each of these animal groups has many thousands of different species. Some animals move from one place to another to find food, warmth, or shelter. This is called migration.

Atlantic Ocean

Magellanic penguin

4

Leopard seal

4

A   B   C

D   **E**   **F**

Arctic Ocean

Reindeer

Steppe polecat

Fox

EUROPE

Chamois

ASIA

Tiger

Cobra

Elephant

Octopus

AFRICA

Hippo

Giraffe

Pacific Ocean

Green turtle

EQUATOR

Orangutan

Lion

Flying fish

AUSTRALIA

Zebra

Indian Ocean

Dingo

Wallaby

Koala

Kiwi

Blue whale

ANTARCTIC CIRCLE

ANTARCTICA

1

2

3

4

5

Monarch butterflies spend the winter in the southern U.S. and Mexico. In the summer, they migrate thousands of miles north, to the northern U.S. and Canada.

Can you find one on the map?

CANADA AND ALASKA

Northern Canada and Alaska are inside
the Arctic Circle, where it is freezing cold.
This snowy wasteland is called the tundra.
Further to the south, there are tall mountains,
grassy plains, and big lakes. Many animals
live in each of these different habitats.

Arctic tern

Snow geese

Polar bear

Arctic fox

ALASKA (U.S.)

Yukon

YUKON
TERRITORY

Mackenzie

Moose

Walrus

Caribou

Dall sheep

NORTHWEST
TERRITORIES

King salmon

Sea otter

ALBERTA

Rocky Mountains

Grizzly bear

Fur seal

Pacific
Ocean

Pacific salmon

BRITISH
COLUMBIA

Bald eagle

Gray whales

0

0

1000km

500 miles

D

E

F

1

2

Arctic hare

Narwhal

Grizzly bears live in cold places, in forests, and on mountains and tundra. In the winter, they dig dens, where they hibernate, or sleep.

Can you find one on the map?

Ringed seal

Polar bear

Musk ox

Whistling swan

Lemming

NUNAVUT

Canada goose

ARCTIC CIRCLE

Arctic wolf

Caribou

Atlantic Ocean

3

CANADA

Snowy owl

Beluga whale

Hudson Bay

Hooded seal

SASKATCHEWAN

MANITOBA

Wolverine

NEWFOUNDLAND AND LABRADOR

Dairy cow

Beaver

ONTARIO

Black bear

QUÉBEC

St. Lawrence

NEW BRUNSWICK

PRINCE EDWARD ISLAND

Cod

4

Skunk

Blue jay

NOVA SCOTIA

7

D

E

F

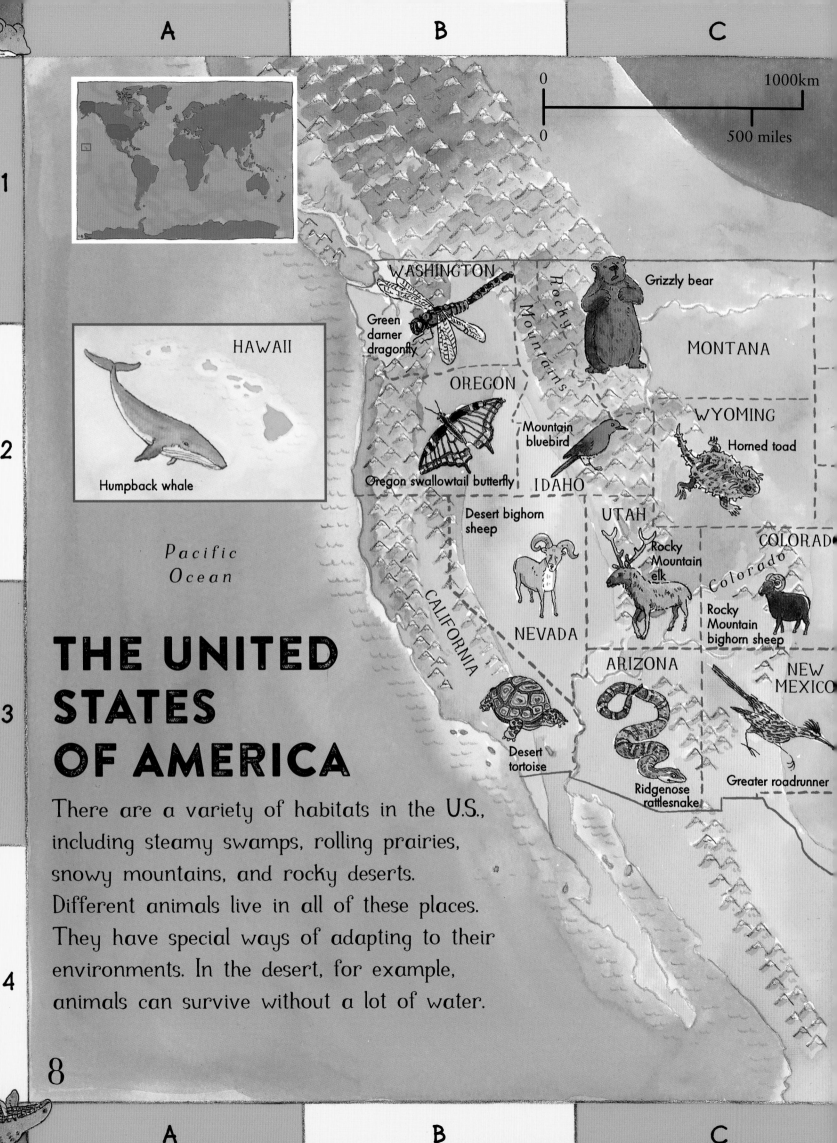

1000km

0

0

500 miles

1

2

3

4

WASHINGTON

Grizzly bear

Green darner dragonfly

Rocky Mountains

MONTANA

OREGON

WYOMING

Mountain bluebird

Horned toad

Oregon swallowtail butterfly

IDAHO

UTAH

COLORADO

Desert bighorn sheep

Rocky Mountain elk

Colorado

HAWAII

Rocky Mountain bighorn sheep

Humpback whale

NEVADA

Pacific Ocean

CALIFORNIA

ARIZONA

NEW MEXICO

THE UNITED STATES OF AMERICA

Desert tortoise

Ridgenose rattlesnake

Greater roadrunner

There are a variety of habitats in the U.S., including steamy swamps, rolling prairies, snowy mountains, and rocky deserts. Different animals live in all of these places. They have special ways of adapting to their environments. In the desert, for example, animals can survive without a lot of water.

8

Every time a **rattlesnake** sheds its skin, a new piece is added onto its tail. This is why older rattlesnakes are noisier than young ones!

Can you find one on the map?

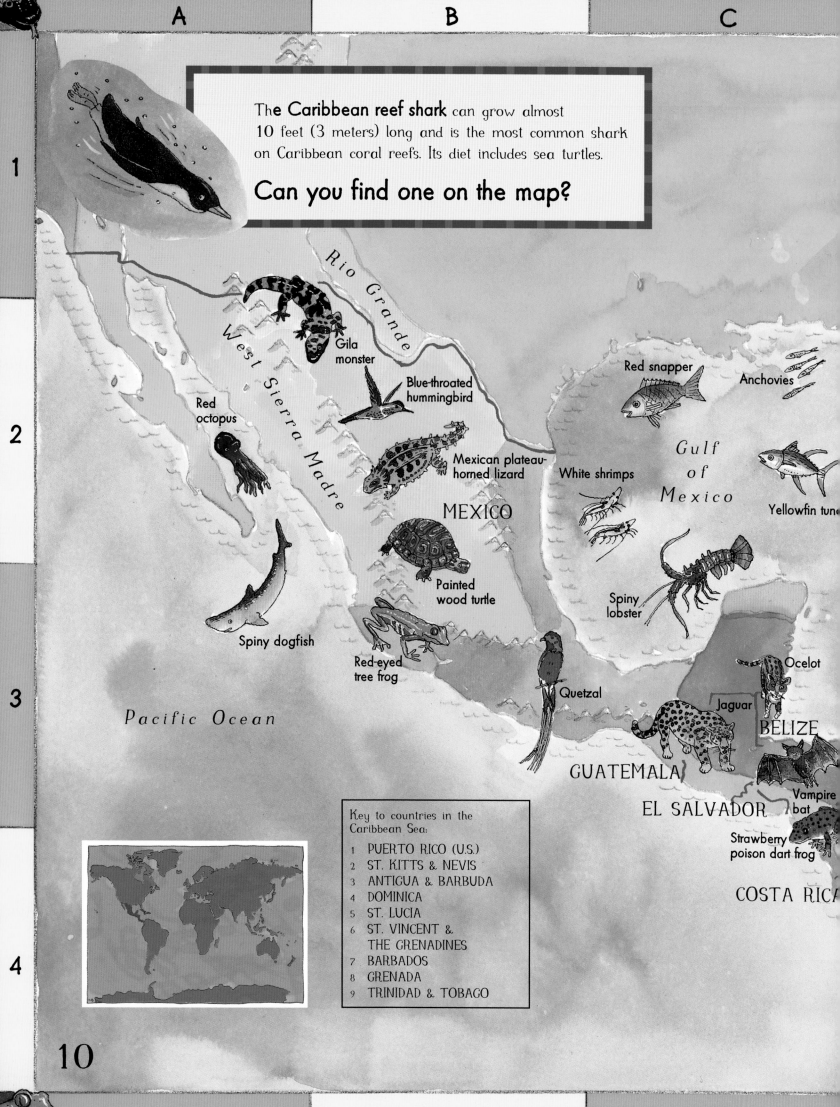

The **Caribbean reef shark** can grow almost 10 feet (3 meters) long and is the most common shark on Caribbean coral reefs. Its diet includes sea turtles.

Can you find one on the map?

Rio Grande

West Sierra Madre

Gila monster

Blue-throated hummingbird

Red octopus

Mexican plateau-horned lizard

Red snapper

Anchovies

Gulf of Mexico

White shrimps

Yellowfin tuna

MEXICO

Painted wood turtle

Spiny lobster

Spiny dogfish

Red-eyed tree frog

Quetzal

Ocelot

Jaguar

BELIZE

GUATEMALA

Vampire bat

Pacific Ocean

EL SALVADOR

Strawberry poison dart frog

COSTA RICA

Key to countries in the Caribbean Sea:

1 PUERTO RICO (U.S.)
2 ST. KITTS & NEVIS
3 ANTIGUA & BARBUDA
4 DOMINICA
5 ST. LUCIA
6 ST. VINCENT &
   THE GRENADINES
7 BARBADOS
8 GRENADA
9 TRINIDAD & TOBAGO

MEXICO, CENTRAL AMERICA, AND THE CARIBBEAN

There are dry deserts in northern Mexico and wet rainforests in Central America. Not many creatures are able to survive in the scorching desert, but an amazing number of animals and plants live in tropical rain forests. To the east, the Caribbean Sea is famous for its coral reefs, which are home to a colorful collection of marine creatures.

BAHAMAS

West Indian flamingo

Rhinoceros iguana

Atlantic Ocean

Spotted dolphin

Stingray

CUBA

JAMAICA

DOMINICAN REPUBLIC

HAITI

Marine toad

Frigate bird

Jamaican white peacock butterfly

HONDURAS

West Indian manatee

Green turtle

Caribbean reef shark

Sisserou parrot

Caribbean Sea

NICARAGUA

Swordfish

Puffer fish

St. Vincent parrot

Keel-billed toucan

Clown fish

PANAMA

Howler monkey

White-tail sabre wing hummingbird

Spider monkey

0   1000km

0   500 miles

11

ROCKY DESERT

The deserts of the western U.S. are very dry and hot. Not many plants can grow in these harsh conditions. The animals that survive in this habitat have special ways of hunting and of protecting themselves from the fierce heat.

When it is attacked, the **western banded gecko** can deliberately "lose" its tail. The predator eats the tail while the gecko runs away.

The **greater roadrunner** is the size of a chicken. It can run at 25 miles per hour (40 km/hr).

When the **chuckwalla** hides between rocks, it puffs out its body so that it cannot be dragged out by a predator.

When a **western diamondback rattlesnake** shakes its tail, the tip rattles!

The **Gila monster** is a dangerous lizard. It squirts poison through its teeth.

Desert tortoise

12

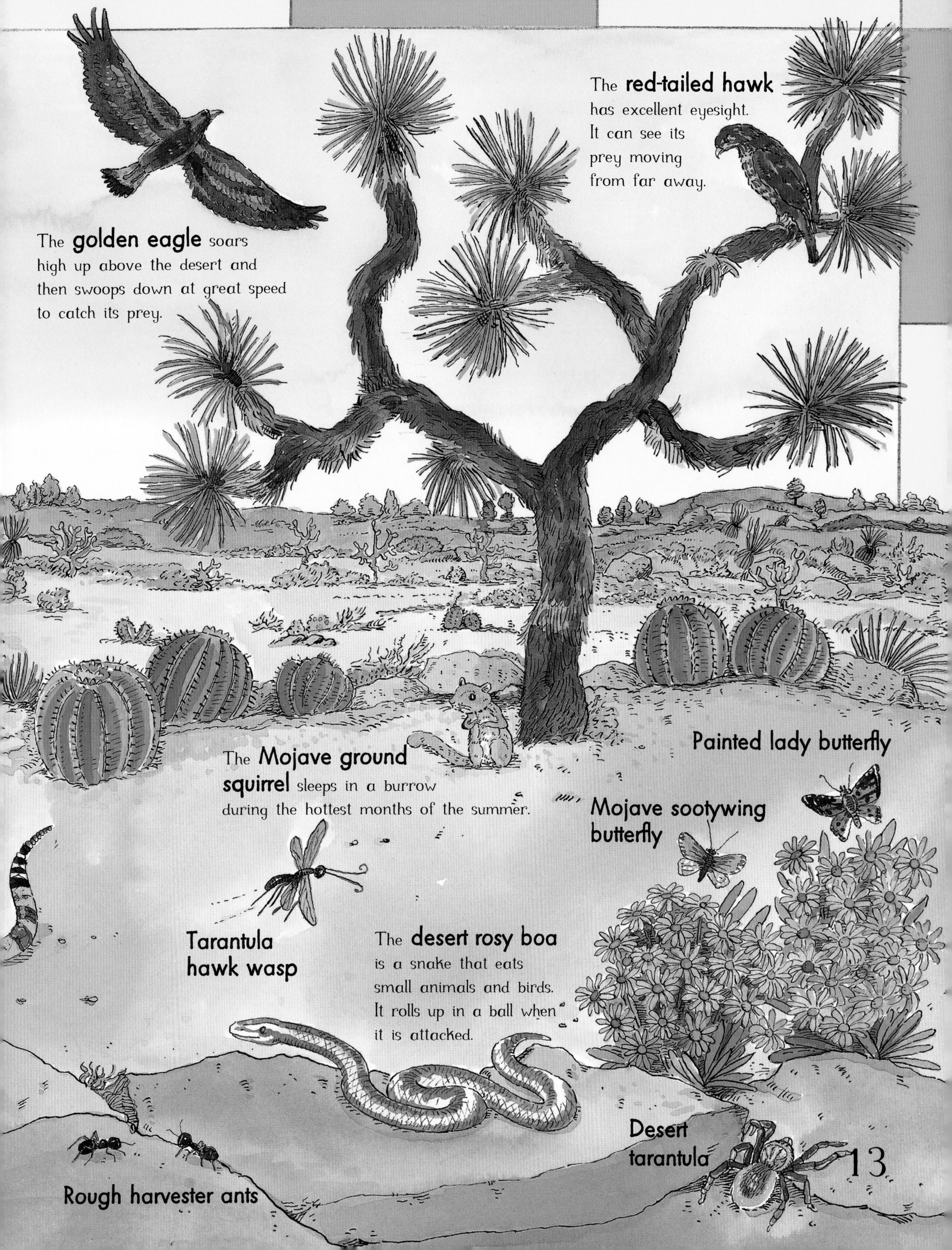

The **red-tailed hawk** has excellent eyesight. It can see its prey moving from far away.

The **golden eagle** soars high up above the desert and then swoops down at great speed to catch its prey.

The **Mojave ground squirrel** sleeps in a burrow during the hottest months of the summer.

Painted lady butterfly

Mojave sootywing butterfly

Tarantula hawk wasp

The **desert rosy boa** is a snake that eats small animals and birds. It rolls up in a ball when it is attacked.

Desert tarantula

Rough harvester ants

13

14

SOUTH AMERICA

South America has a variety of habitats. The Amazon rain forest contains more species than anywhere else on Earth. The Andes, the world's longest mountain range, is home to many different animals. The southern grasslands are also rich in wildlife.

The **Andean condor** is one of the world's heaviest flying birds, weighing up to 33 pounds (15 kilograms). Amazingly, it can spot another condor 6 miles (9 kilometers) away.

Can you find one?

1000km

500 miles

0

0

Atlantic Ocean

Pacific Ocean

URUGUAY

Sheep

ARGENTINA

Rhea

Cattle

Alpaca

CHILE

Pampas deer

Patagonia

Falkland Islands (U.K.)

Magellanic penguin

Sea lion

Fur seal

Sardines

4

5

6

A

B

C

D

RAINFOREST

The Amazon rainforest is very hot and also extremely wet—it rains for around 250 days each year. This combination is perfect for both plant and animal life, and this is why the rain forest is home to so many different species.

The colorful beak of the **toco toucan** is almost as big as the bird itself. It is mostly made of lightweight bone.

Blue morpho butterflies have bright blue wings. They flash when they catch the sunlight.

The **black caiman** is a big, dangerous alligator that preys on large animals, including humans.

Green iguana

The steamy rain forest climate is ideal for frogs. The **poison dart frog** has bright colors to warn predators to stay away.

Longhorn beetles have two antennae that can be longer than their bodies.

Scarlet macaw

Red howler monkeys

Tree kinkajou

The **two-toed sloth** eats, sleeps, and even gives birth upside down!

Emerald tree boa

The world's largest rodent is the **capybara**. It is more than 3 feet (1 meter) long and almost 20 inches (50 centimeters) tall.

The spotted fur of the **jaguar** helps it hide in the shadows of the rainforest.

The strange **matamata turtle** snaps up small creatures as they float or swim by.

Giant otters can stay underwater for several minutes. Their sensitive whiskers help them find prey in the murky river.

17

1 2 3

A B C D

Killer whale

ARCTIC CIRCLE

Wolverine

Wolf

FINLAND

Trout

European mink

ESTONIA

Beaver

LATVIA

LITHUANIA

White stork

Baltic Sea

Guillemot

Reindeer

SWEDEN

Lynx

Moose

Badger

Eurasian otter

Fjord pony

NORWAY

Sheep

400km

250 miles

0

0

Herring

Salmon

Pig

DENMARK

Dairy cow

Gray seals

North Sea

ARCTIC CIRCLE

ICELAND

Arctic fox

NORTHERN AND EASTERN EUROPE

Animals that live in the north of Europe survive well in the cold, snowy pine forests and mountains. Farther south, the climate is warmer, and there is a greater variety of animal species. The wildlife that lives close to the Mediterranean Sea is well suited to that hot climate.

The **reindeer** of northern parts of Norway and Sweden are always on the move in search of food. Large herds swim across freezing rivers and even through the sea between islands.

Can you find one on the map?

European bison

Deer

CZECH REPUBLIC

POLAND

Muskrat

Tiger moth

SLOVAKIA

HUNGARY

Heron

Ibex

European hare

Danube

ROMANIA

Deer

Wild boar

SLOVENIA

CROATIA

BOSNIA & HERZEGOVINA

Garden dormouse

Sturgeon

MONTENEGRO

SERBIA

Brown bear

Danube

BULGARIA

Black Sea

ALBANIA

NORTH MACEDONIA

Lesser horseshoe bat

Goat

Marginated tortoise

GREECE

Bottle-nosed dolphin

Mediterranean Sea

Vistula

19

WESTERN EUROPE

Europe is a small continent with many different animal habitats. Wildlife is found everywhere, from cool, shady woodlands to hot, dry plains. Animals have also adapted to life in the high mountains of central and southern Europe.

Gray squirrels were brought to the U.K. from the U.S. in the 1800s. They are now more common than the smaller red squirrel.

Can you find one on the map?

Baltic Sea

North Sea

Cod

Plaice

NETHERLANDS

Western European hedgehog

Avocet

Gray squirrel

Highland cattle

SCOTLAND

UNITED KINGDOM

NORTHERN IRELAND

Sheep

Gray seal

Haddock

Horse

IRELAND

20

A   B   C   D

1   2   3

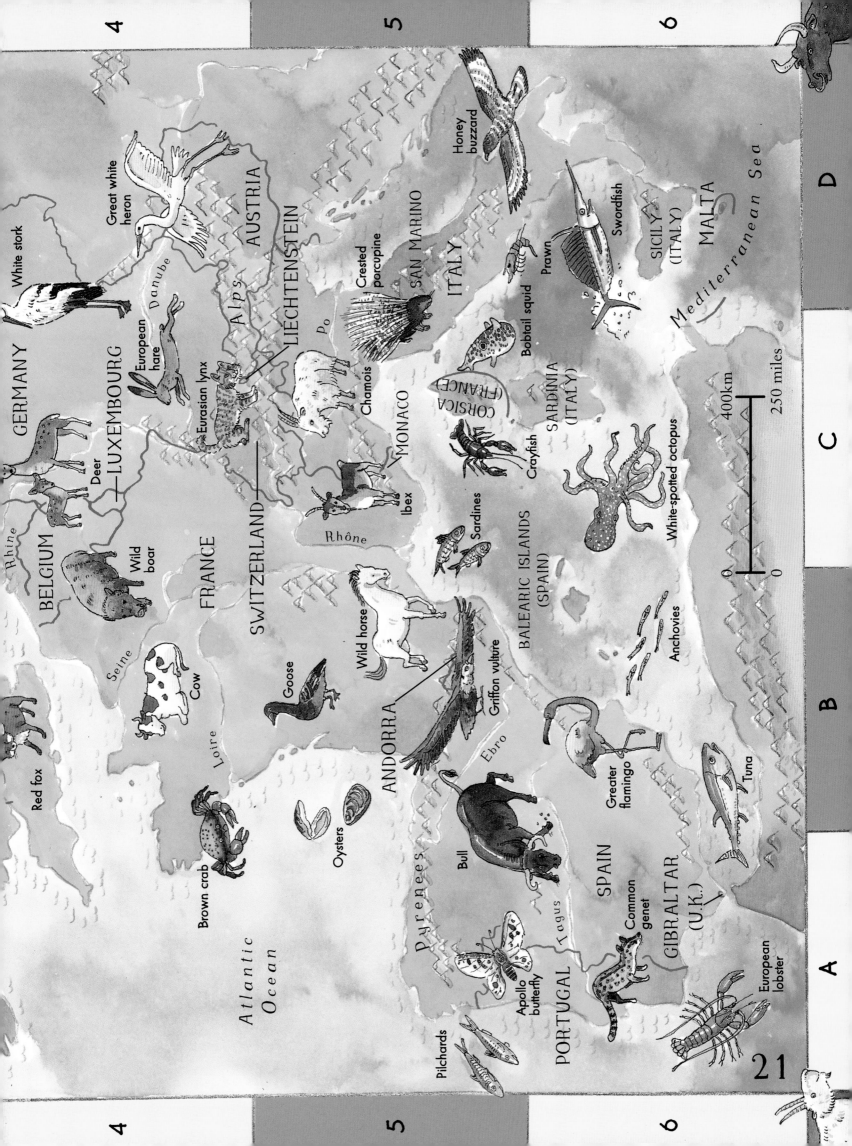

WOODLAND

Trees that lose their leaves in the winter are called deciduous. Woods of deciduous trees, like this one in Europe, are home to many different animals, birds, and insects. Each woodland creature has a special job to do, such as spreading seeds.

Long-eared bat

Only the male **blackbird** is black— the female is brown. Blackbirds eat insects, worms, and berries.

Garden spider

Red admiral butterfly

Common shrew

The **adder** likes to bask in the sun in woodland clearings.

The **red fox** usually hunts at night. It eats nuts and berries, as well as small forest creatures.

22

Earthworm

Green woodpecker

Tawny owl

In fall, the
gray squirrel
buries food
underground.
It digs it
up again in
the winter.

A **robin** fights other
robins in order to
protect its territory.
It will even attack its
own reflection!

Badger

The **garden snail** retreats into
its shell when the weather is dry.
It can then live for several
months without water.

Wood mouse

The **hedgehog** is usually
active at night. During the day,
it curls into a ball to sleep.

Wood lice

23

RUSSIA AND ITS NEIGHBORS

Russia is a huge country, and the wildlife is as varied as the landscape. Frozen tundra, pine forests, and mountain ranges are home to many different creatures. In countries south of Russia, the climate is drier, and tough animals survive in the high-lying deserts.

Arctic Ocean

Collared lemming

Polar bear

Arctic cod

Canada goose

Yenisey

ARCTIC CIRCLE

Lynx

Moose

Reindeer

Ural Mountains

Golden eagle

Russian flying squirrel

Ob

KALININGRAD

Steppe polecat

Volga

Honeybee

Snow leopard

Red fox

Domestic pig

BELARUS

Saiga antelope

Ural

Wild boar

KAZAKHSTAN

Caspian seal

Bactrian camel

MOLDOVA

Chamois

UKRAINE

Black Sea

Caspian Sea

UZBEKISTAN

GEORGIA

ARMENIA

KYRGYZSTAN

TAJIKISTAN

AZERBAIJAN

Jackal

TURKMENISTAN

24

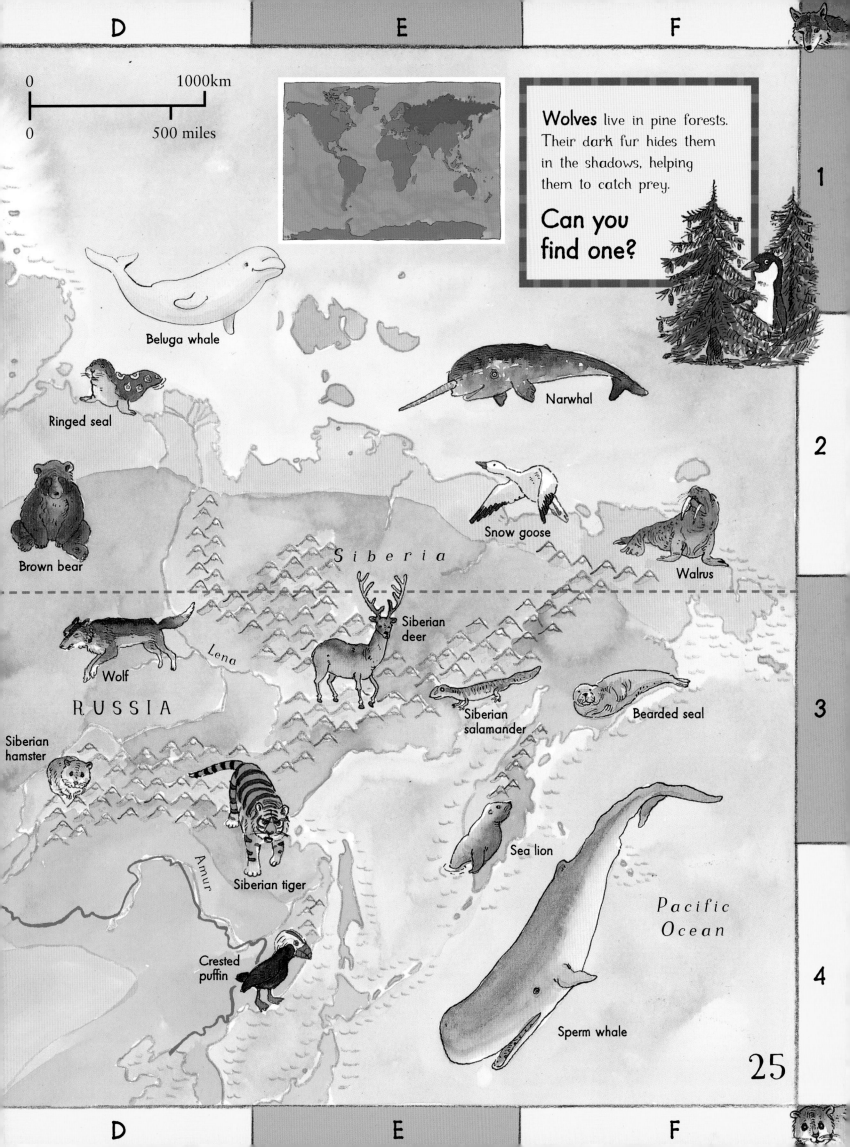

1000km

500 miles

Wolves live in pine forests. Their dark fur hides them in the shadows, helping them to catch prey.

Can you find one?

Beluga whale

Narwhal

Ringed seal

Snow goose

S i b e r i a

Walrus

Brown bear

Siberian deer

Wolf

Lena

Siberian salamander

Bearded seal

R U S S I A

Siberian hamster

Sea lion

Amur

Siberian tiger

Pacific Ocean

Crested puffin

Sperm whale

25

1

2

SOUTHWESTERN ASIA

Mountain ranges lie to the northeast of this region, but much of southwestern Asia is extremely dry and hot. The deserts in this part of the world are sandy and windy. Few animals can survive in the scorching heat. Those that do are able to live on very little water.

3

Angora goat

Brown bear

TURKEY

Thermit ibis

Wild sheep

CYPRUS

Sand gazelles

SYRIA

Mediterranean Sea

LEBANON

Wild boar

ISRAEL

JORDAN

Turkish gecko

Dromedary camel

Fennec fox

Dugong

Hamadryas baboon

Tiger shark

Red Sea

Hawksbill turtle

The **dromedary camel** can go without water for a week. When it does drink, it can gulp down up to 52 gallons (200 liters) of water in one go.

Can you find one on the map?

4

26

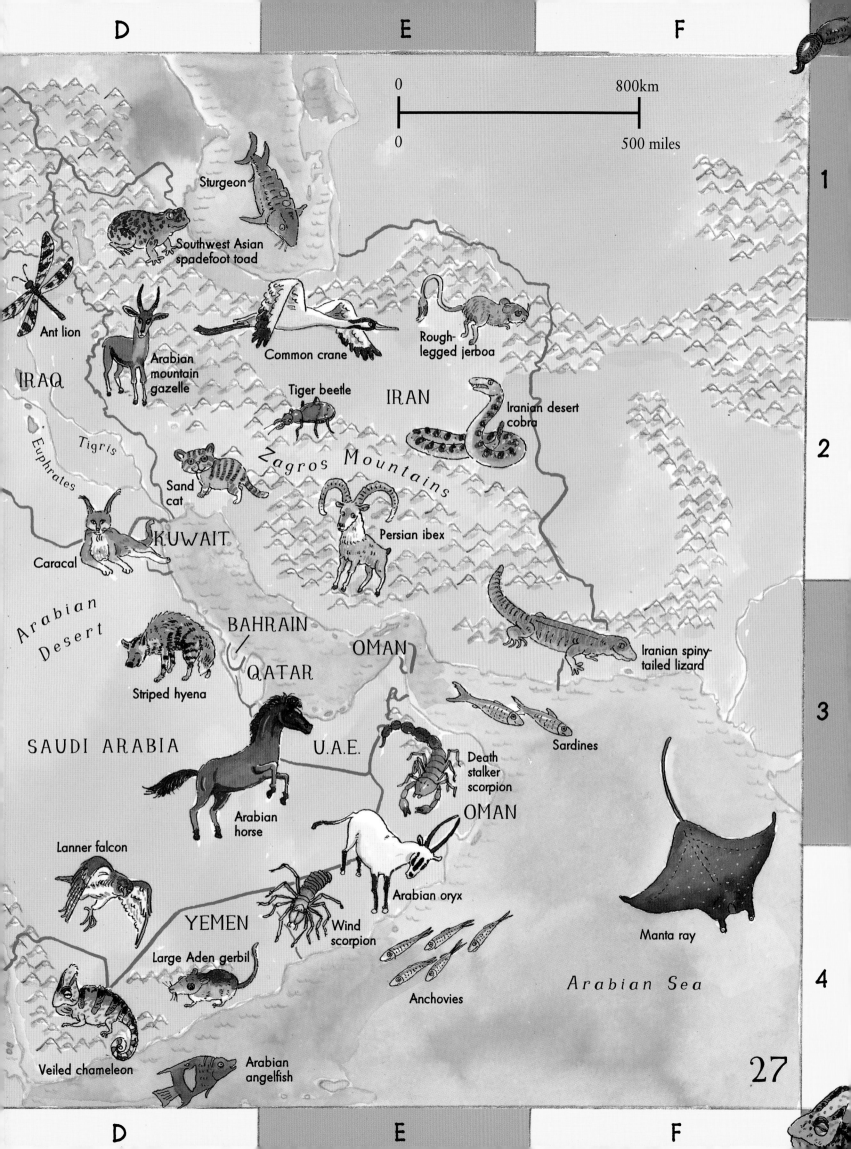

D   E   F

0   800km

0   500 miles

1

Sturgeon

Southwest Asian
spadefoot toad

Ant lion

Arabian
mountain
gazelle

Common crane

Rough-
legged jerboa

IRAQ

Tigris

Euphrates

Tiger beetle

IRAN

Iranian desert
cobra

2

Sand
cat

Zagros Mountains

KUWAIT

Caracal

Persian ibex

Arabian
Desert

BAHRAIN

OMAN

Iranian spiny-
tailed lizard

QATAR

Striped hyena

Sardines

3

SAUDI ARABIA

U.A.E.

Death
stalker
scorpion

OMAN

Arabian
horse

Lanner falcon

Arabian oryx

Manta ray

YEMEN

Wind
scorpion

Large Aden gerbil

Anchovies

Arabian Sea

4

Veiled chameleon

Arabian
angelfish

27

D   E   F

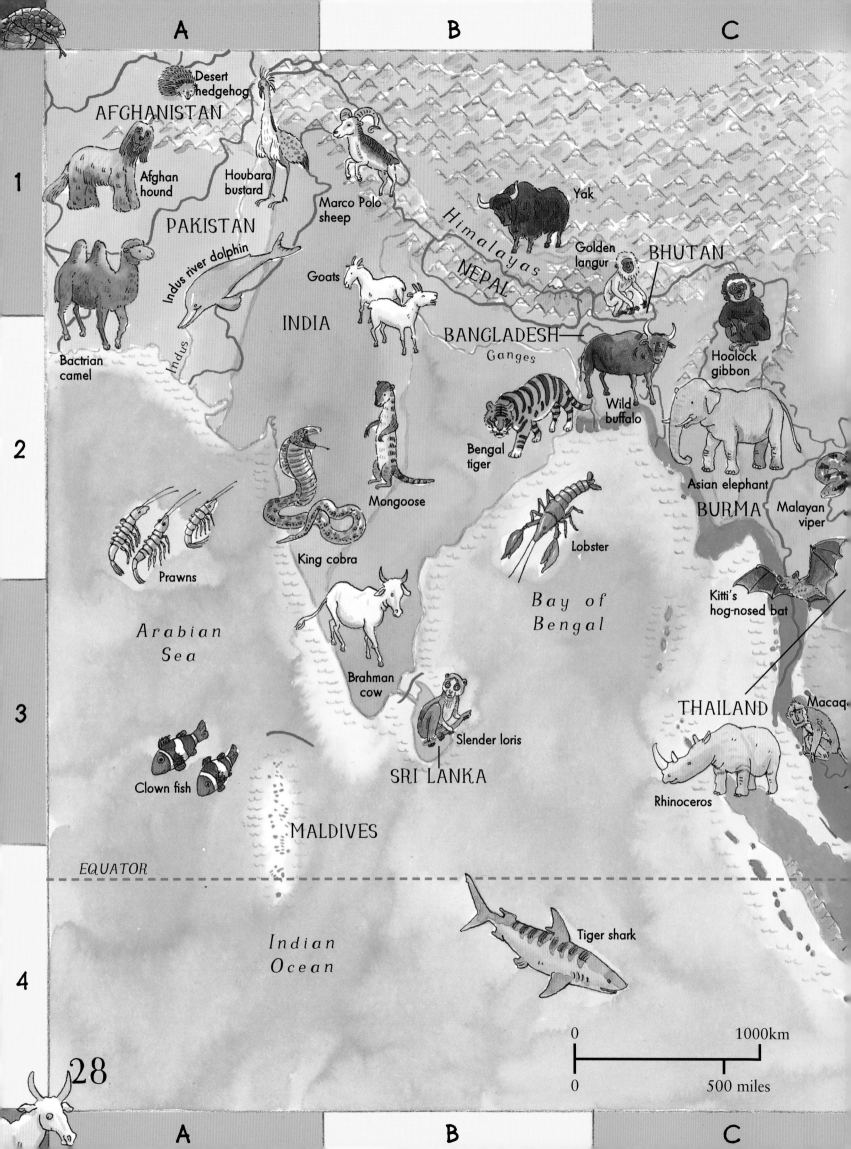

Desert hedgehog

AFGHANISTAN

Afghan hound

Houbara bustard

Marco Polo sheep

1

Yak

Golden langur

BHUTAN

PAKISTAN

NEPAL

Indus river dolphin

Goats

Hoolock gibbon

INDIA

BANGLADESH

Ganges

Indus

Bactrian camel

Wild buffalo

Asian elephant

Mongoose

Bengal tiger

BURMA

Malayan viper

2

King cobra

Lobster

Prawns

Bay of Bengal

Kitti's hog-nosed bat

Arabian Sea

Brahman cow

THAILAND

Macaq

3

Slender loris

SRI LANKA

Rhinoceros

Clown fish

MALDIVES

Tiger shark

Indian Ocean

4

0   1000km

0   500 miles

SOUTHERN AND SOUTHEASTERN ASIA

A huge mountain range called the Himalayas lies to the north of this region. Countries south of the Himalayas are very hot, and those close to the equator have a tropical climate. Most of Indonesia is covered with thick rainforest, which is home to a wide variety of wildlife.

1

The **Komodo dragon** is the world's biggest lizard, and it looks like a living dinosaur. It grows up to 10 feet (3 meters) long.

Can you find one?

2

Asiatic black bear

VIETNAM

South China Sea

Draco lizard

LAOS

Clouded leopard

Manta ray

PHILIPPINES

CAMBODIA

MALAYSIA

3

Pacific Ocean

SINGAPORE

Tarsier

Philippine cockatoo

Hornbill

BRUNEI

Giant palm civet

Leatherback turtle

Orangutans

INDONESIA

Queen Alexandra birdwing butterfly

4

Malayan tapir

Komodo dragon

EAST TIMOR

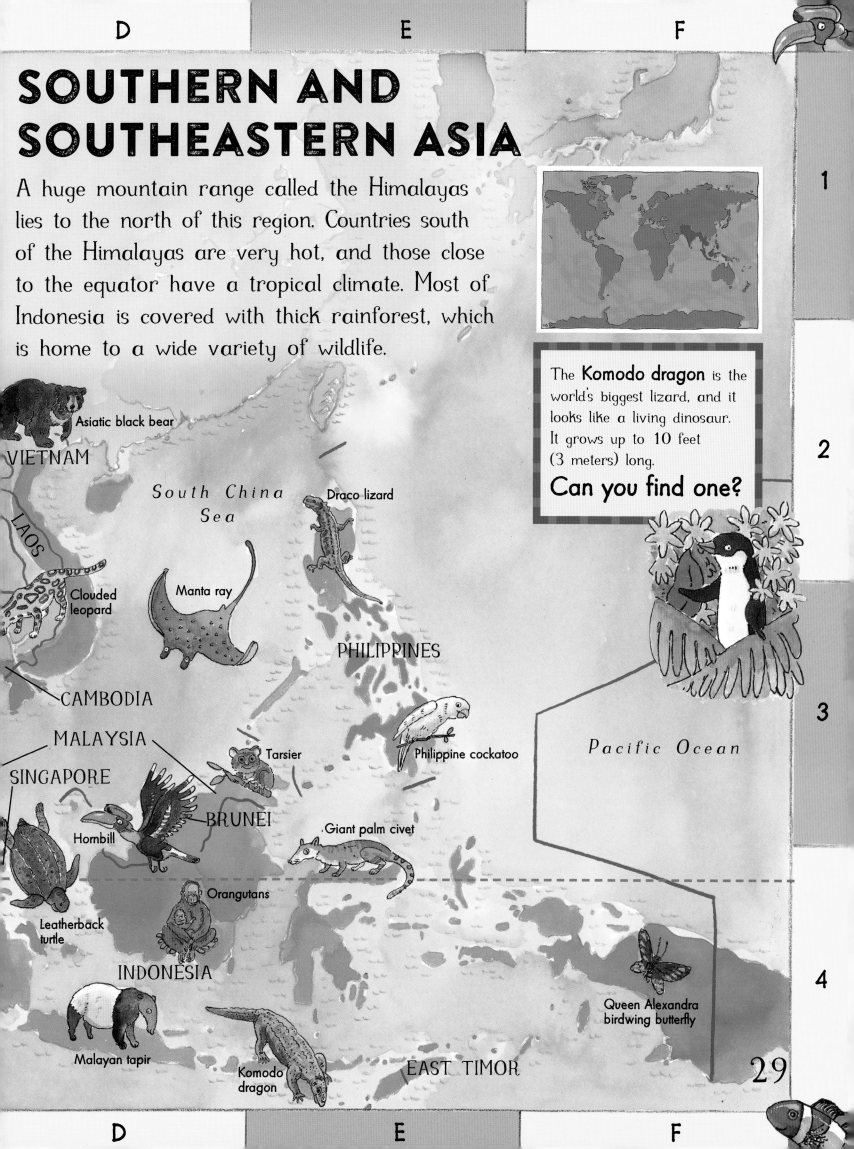

THE HIMALAYAS

The Himalayas form the biggest range, or group, of mountains in the world. Fourteen of the world's tallest mountains are found in the Himalayas. The sturdy animals that live there are well adapted to life on the high slopes.

Musk deer

The **bharal** lives in small herds and is preyed on by snow leopards.

The **Himalayan brown bear** lives high up the mountain in the summer, when it is not too cold to survive up there.

Himalayan weasel

When a male **rock agama** fights another male, he will try to hit the other lizard on the head with his tail!

Himalayan pika

The **bearded vulture** builds its nest high up on craggy mountain rocks. It feeds on dead animals, dropping the bones in order to smash them and get to the tasty marrow inside.

Red-billed
blue magpie

Himalayan
yellow-throated marten

The **yak** is a wild mountain ox. It climbs around 20,000 feet (6,100 meters) up the mountain to feed. An adult male can weigh as much as ten humans.

Snow leopards can live higher up than any other wildcat. When they sleep, they wrap their tails around their bodies to stay warm.

Marmot

Swallowtail butterfly

The male **Himalayan monal pheasant** is brightly colored and has a crest of feathers on its head. The smaller female has no crest and is brown in color.

31

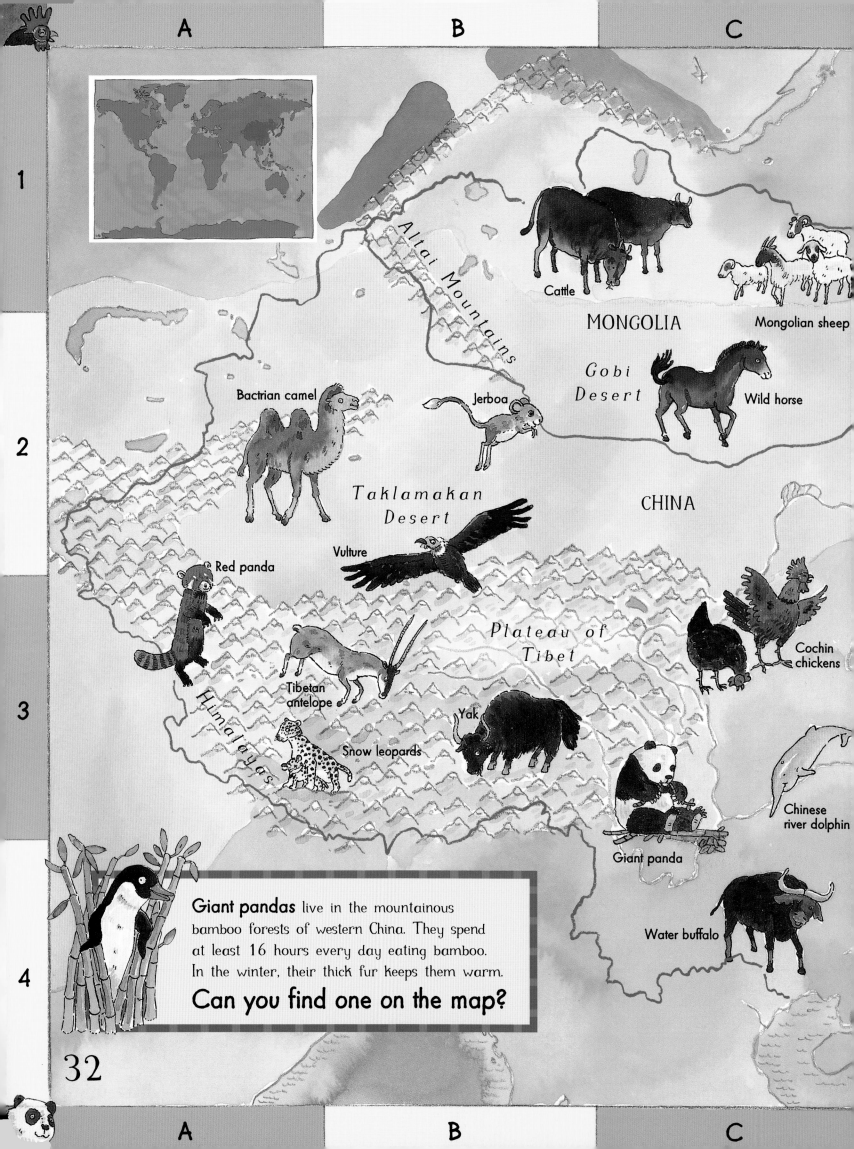

1

MONGOLIA

Cattle

Mongolian sheep

Altai Mountains

Bactrian camel

Jerboa

Gobi
Desert

Wild horse

2

Taklamakan
Desert

CHINA

Vulture

Red panda

Plateau of
Tibet

Cochin
chickens

Tibetan
antelope

Yak

Himalayas

Snow leopards

Giant panda

Chinese
river dolphin

3

Giant pandas live in the mountainous
bamboo forests of western China. They spend
at least 16 hours every day eating bamboo.
In the winter, their thick fur keeps them warm.

Can you find one on the map?

Water buffalo

32

4

0   1000km

0   500 miles

1

Black bear

Siberian tiger

Nen Jiang

Dhole

Harlequin duck

House swallow

2

Steller's sea eagle

NORTH KOREA

Squid

Japanese macaque

Whooper swan

Pacific Ocean

SOUTH KOREA

Crane

JAPAN

Huang He (Yellow river)

Siberian musk deer

Chinese alligator

CHINA AND JAPAN

3

Octopus

Chang Jiang (Yangtze)

Chinese moon moth

Emerald green tree frog

As well as having the world's biggest human population, China is also home to many amazing species of wild animals. A wide variety of creatures live in the mountains to the south and the high-lying deserts to the north. The seas around Japan and North and South Korea are full of interesting marine life.

Gibbon

TAIWAN

Unicorn beetle

4

Dugong

33

1   2   3

D   C   B   A

Saharan horned viper

MOROCCO

Sheep

WESTERN SAHARA

Senegal parrot

MAURITANIA

Dromedary camel

Addax

Cattle

MALI

ALGERIA

Rock rabbit

Sahara Desert

Sand cat

LIBYA

Desert scorpion

Striped hyena

TUNISIA

Mediterranean Sea

EGYPT

Nile crocodile

Nile

Sand fox

Gerbil

CHAD

NIGER

NIGERIA

African gray parrot

Aardvark

Niger

Barbary shrike

Hawksbill turtle

GUINEA

SIERRA LEONE

IVORY COAST

LIBERIA

West African manatee

CAMEROON

Giant forest hog

GABON

CONGO

ANGOLA (CABINDA)

Chimpanzee

Mountain gorilla

Forest buffalo

Hippopotamus

Grant's gazelle

UGANDA

SOUTH SUDAN

White rhinoceros

SUDAN

KENYA

Cheetah

Bush baby

ETHIOPIA

SOMALIA

Ethiopian wolf

Eland

DJIBOUTI

ERITREA

Red Sea

EQUATOR

1000km

500 miles

0   0

1   4   5   6   7   8   9   10   11   12   13

1   2   3

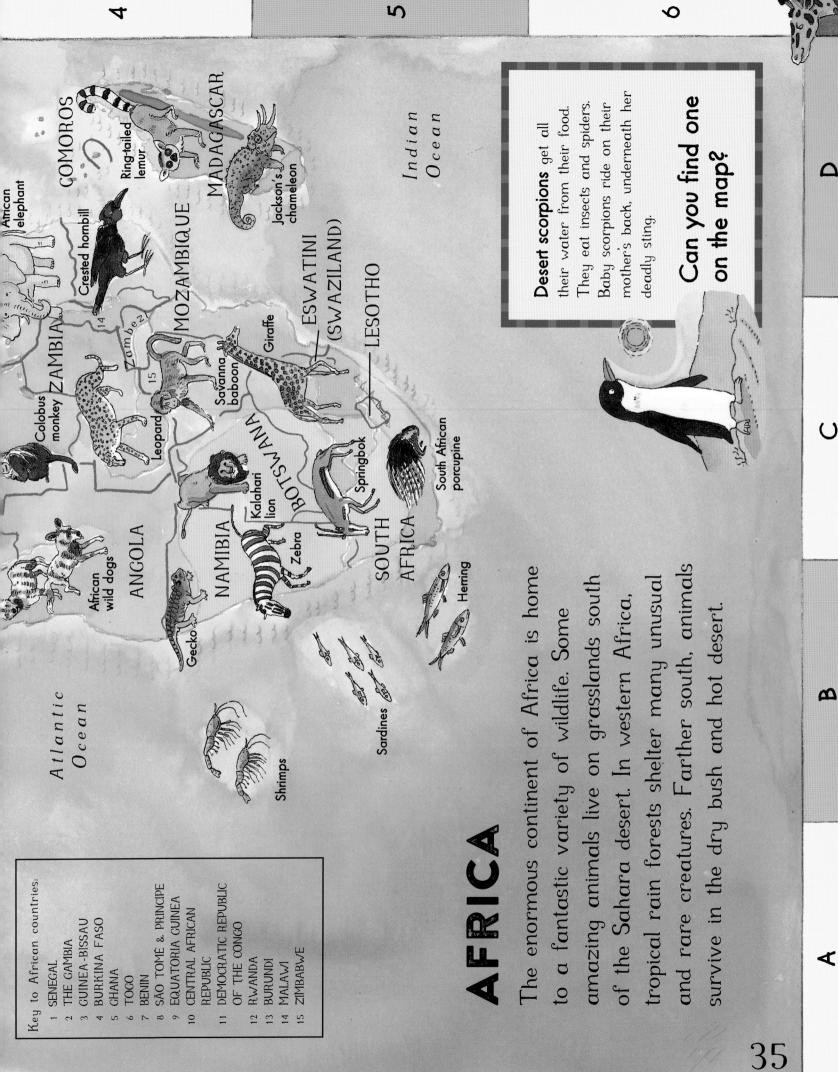

AFRICA

The enormous continent of Africa is home to a fantastic variety of wildlife. Some amazing animals live on grasslands south of the Sahara desert. In western Africa, tropical rain forests shelter many unusual and rare creatures. Farther south, animals survive in the dry bush and hot desert.

Key to African countries:
1   SENEGAL
2   THE GAMBIA
3   GUINEA-BISSAU
4   BURKINA FASO
5   GHANA
6   TOGO
7   BENIN
8   SÃO TOMÉ & PRÍNCIPE
9   EQUATORIAL GUINEA
10 CENTRAL AFRICAN
    REPUBLIC
11 DEMOCRATIC REPUBLIC
    OF THE CONGO
12 RWANDA
13 BURUNDI
14 MALAWI
15 ZIMBABWE

Desert scorpions get all their water from their food. They eat insects and spiders. Baby scorpions ride on their mother's back, underneath her deadly sting.

Can you find one on the map?

COMOROS

MADAGASCAR

Ring-tailed lemur

African elephant

Crested hornbill

Jackson's chameleon

MOZAMBIQUE

ZAMBIA

Colobus monkey

Zambezi

Leopard

Savanna baboon

Giraffe

ESWATINI (SWAZILAND)

LESOTHO

ANGOLA

African wild dogs

NAMIBIA

Gecko

Kalahari lion

BOTSWANA

Springbok

Zebra

SOUTH AFRICA

South African porcupine

Herring

Sardines

Shrimps

Atlantic Ocean

Indian Ocean

4

5

6

A   B   C   D

SAVANNA

The vast grassy plains of Africa are called the savanna. Herds of wild animals, such as gazelles, live in this habitat. They are hunted by lions and other predators.

Giraffes can reach up to the tallest branches to graze on tasty leaves.

Cheetah

Thomson's gazelles live in herds. They are safer from predators if they stay in big groups.

No two **zebras** are exactly alike. Every zebra has its own stripe pattern.

Oxpecker

African bush elephants are bigger than any other elephant. Their size protects them from predators.

Hippopotamus

The **oxpecker** pecks insects off the back of a **hippopotamus**. This is good for both the bird and the hippo.

Dung beetles are useful insects. They clear away and recycle the dung of the huge savanna animals.

The **griffon vulture** never kills its own food. It eats the meat of animals that are already dead.

Savanna baboons

Eastern black-white colobus monkeys shelter from the heat in the shady branches of a tree.

A male **lion** does not hunt as much as a female does. Lions live in groups called prides.

If a **pangolin** is in danger, it rolls up into a ball.

Black rhinoceroses come to water holes to drink.

The **savanna monitor lizard** flicks its forked tongue in and out to find prey. It eats birds, snakes, lizards, and eggs.

The tusks of a male **warthog** can grow up to 25 inches (64 centimeters) long.

1

2

3

4

NORTHERN
TERRITORY

Frilled
lizard

Red
kangaroo

*Great Sandy
Desert*

Dingo

AUSTRALIA

Spiny anteater

WESTERN
AUSTRALIA

SOUTH
AUSTRALIA

Sheep

Thorny devil

Southern
hairy-nosed
wombat

Western
brush wallaby

Great white shark

*Great Australian
Bight*

Sea dragon

Southern right whale

Emu

The **red kangaroo** hops across the grassy
plains of Australia at up to 37 miles
(60 kilometers) per hour. It keeps its balance
by stretching out its long tail.

Can you find one on the map?

AUSTRALIA AND NEW ZEALAND

Some animals that live in this part of the world are not found anywhere else, such as the strange duck-billed platypus of Australia and the flightless kiwi of New Zealand. Animal farming is a big industry in Australia and New Zealand. There are many more sheep than people in both of these countries.

Blacktip reef shark

Butterfly fish

Blue-ringed octopus

Great Barrier Reef

Great Dividing Range

Koala

Duck-billed platypus

QUEENSLAND

Kookaburra

Darling

NEW SOUTH WALES

Blue-tongued skink

AUSTRALIAN CAPITAL TERRITORY

Murray

VICTORIA

Tasman Sea

Tasmanian devil

TASMANIA

Pacific Ocean

Crown of thorns starfish

Scorpion fish

NORTH ISLAND

NEW ZEALAND

Long-tailed bat

Kiwi

SOUTH ISLAND

New Zealand sea lion

0   1000km

0   500 miles

1

2

3

4

THE PACIFIC ISLANDS

Thousands of tiny islands, home to lizards, birds, and insects, are scattered across the South Pacific Ocean. The tropical waters are full of fascinating ocean life.

Flying fish do not actually fly—they glide above the surface of the water on their outstretched fins.

Can you find one on the map?

Key to countries:
1 GUAM (U.S.)
2 PALAU
3 NAURU
4 WALLIS & FUTUNA ISLANDS (FRANCE)
5 TOKELAU (N.Z.)
6 SAMOA
7 AMERICAN SAMOA (U.S.)
8 NIUE (N.Z.)
9 COOK ISLANDS (N.Z.)
10 PITCAIRN ISLANDS (U.K.)

0   1000km
0   500 miles

Long-nosed sea horses

Great hammerhead shark

FRENCH POLYNESIA (FRANCE)

Polynesian gecko

Tahiti petrel

Honeyeater

TONGA

FIJI

Giant squid

Banded iguana

VANUATU

NEW CALEDONIA (FRANCE)

Banks flying fox

SOLOMON ISLANDS

Leatherback turtle

TUVALU

KIRIBATI

South Pacific Ocean

MARSHALL ISLANDS

FEDERATED STATES OF MICRONESIA

Manta ray

Sperm whale

Blue marlin

Flying fish

Stonefish

Anchovies

NORTHERN MARIANA ISLANDS (U.S.)

PAPUA NEW GUINEA

Tree kangaroo

CORAL REEF

Coral reefs are formed with the shells of billions of tiny sea creatures. The Great Barrier Reef, which lies off the coast of northeast Australia, is home to a colorful collection of ocean life.

The **loggerhead turtle** eats clams, crabs, jellyfish, squid, and fish.

Spinner dolphins

Australian brain coral

Mandarin fish

Box jellyfish can grow as big as basketballs. They have a deadly sting.

Barrier reef anemonefish

The poison of the **blue-ringed octopus** can kill an adult human in minutes.

The poisonous **olive sea snake** swims to the surface to breathe.

Blue-spotted fantail ray

The **giant clam** is the world's largest mollusk. Its shell can be 5 feet (1.5 meters) long.

Tubular sponge

Pygmy sea horses

Long-nosed butterfly fish

Sea urchin

Clown fish

Sea cucumber

Blue starfish

Staghorn coral

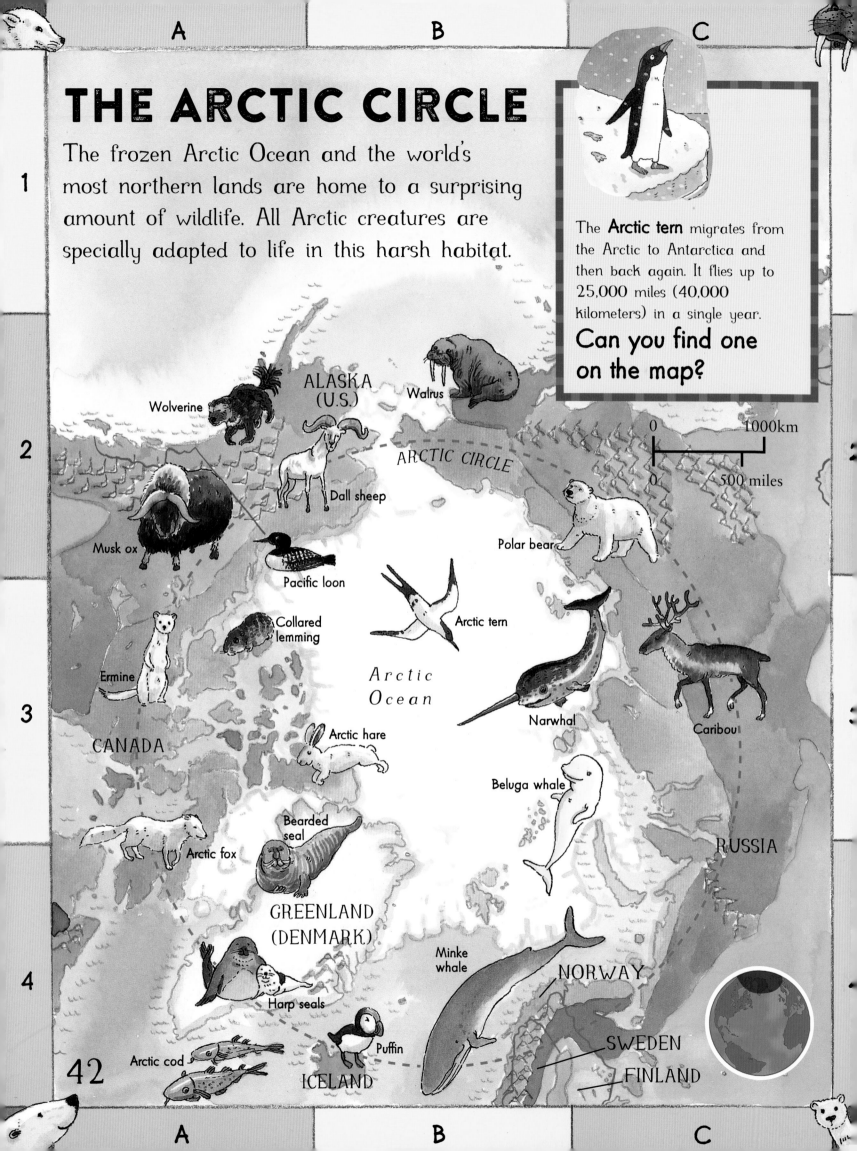

THE ARCTIC CIRCLE

The frozen Arctic Ocean and the world's most northern lands are home to a surprising amount of wildlife. All Arctic creatures are specially adapted to life in this harsh habitat.

The **Arctic tern** migrates from the Arctic to Antarctica and then back again. It flies up to 25,000 miles (40,000 kilometers) in a single year.

Can you find one on the map?

0   1000km

0   500 miles

Wolverine

ALASKA (U.S.)

Walrus

ARCTIC CIRCLE

Dall sheep

Musk ox

Polar bear

Pacific loon

Collared lemming

Arctic tern

Arctic Ocean

Ermine

Narwhal

Caribou

CANADA

Arctic hare

Beluga whale

RUSSIA

Bearded seal

Arctic fox

GREENLAND (DENMARK)

Minke whale

NORWAY

Harp seals

Puffin

SWEDEN

Arctic cod

ICELAND

FINLAND

ANTARCTICA

The continent of Antarctica is so cold that not many living things can survive there. Whales, sharks, and seals swim in the freezing waters, and penguins huddle together on the edges of the ice.

The **emperor penguin** spends most of its time in the freezing Antarctic waters, but it breeds on the ice. The male keeps the egg warm until it hatches.

Can you find one?

Atlantic Ocean

Killer whale

Indian Ocean

Wandering albatross

Giant petrel

Antarctic cod

ANTARCTICA

Blue-eyed shag

Weddell seal

Greater Antarctica

Chinstrap penguin

Lesser Antarctica

Ross seal

Emperor penguins

Pacific Ocean

Minke whale

Adélie penguin

0   1000km

0   500 miles

ANTARCTIC CIRCLE

43

THE ARCTIC

Very few plants grow in the freezing lands of the Arctic. A treeless plain, called the tundra, stretches out in all directions. At the coast, icy seawater laps against bare rocks and ice. Arctic animals have developed clever ways to stay safe and warm in their cold environment.

The **narwhal** is a type of whale. Its tusk grows up to 10 feet (3 meters) long—around half the length of its body and tail.

Beluga whale

The **walrus** has long tusks that it hooks onto ice so that it can sleep in the water.

Ringed seals are the most common seals in the Arctic. They are hunted by polar bears.

Northern collared lemmings

Arctic terns have strong wings that measure up to 33 inches (84 centimeters) from tip to tip.

Unlike most owl species, the **snowy owl** is active during the daytime. Its legs and feet are covered in feathers to protect it from the cold.

Peary caribou

Arctic hares have white fur to help them hide in the snow.

The **Arctic fox** shelters in a rocky den. Some dens have been used for hundreds of years by generations of foxes.

A layer of fat under the fur of **polar bears** means that they can swim in the freezing ocean.

45

GLOSSARY

amphibian
An animal born in water that lives on land.

antenna (pl: antennae)
A feeler or horn.

burrow
A hole or tunnel where an animal lives.

climate
Usual weather in a place.

continent
One of Earth's seven huge blocks of land.

coral reef
A living marine structure, formed with the shells of tiny sea creatures.

deciduous
A plant that loses its leaves in winter.

den
A sheltered place.

desert
A large area of dry land.

diet
Food that is usually eaten by a living thing.

dung
The waste from an animal's body.

environment
Natural surroundings.

Equator
An imaginary line around the middle of Earth.

fin
The thin, flat part of a fish's body.

flightless
Unable to fly.

glide
To fly without flapping.

graze
To eat grass or leaves.

habitat
An animal's home.

herd
A group of animals.

hibernate
To sleep all winter.

mammal
A warm-blooded animal that feeds its babies on milk.

marine
From the ocean.

marrow
The soft insides of bones.

migration
Making the same journey at the same time every year.

mollusk
An animal with a soft body and hard shell.

plain
A flat, treeless area.

prairie
Flat grassland in North America.

predator
An animal that hunts and eats other animals.

prey
An animal that is hunted and eaten by another animal.

rainforest
Tropical forest with a hot, wet climate.

reptile
A cold-blooded animal that creeps or crawls.

rodent
An animal with big front teeth that it uses to chew.

school
A group of marine animals.

species
A set of animals or plants with the same features.

swamp
A marsh or bog.

tentacles
The long, bendy parts of an animal, used for gripping, feeling, or moving.

territory
An area of land that belongs to an animal.

tropical
An area near the Equator with hot weather.

tundra
A treeless, frozen plain.

tusk
A long tooth that pokes out of an animal's mouth.

venom
Poison used to kill prey.

wingspan
The distance between wingtips.

46

INDEX

dep. territory = dependent territory